AMAZING BODY SYSTEMS

SKELETAL SYSTEM

by Karen Latchana Kenney

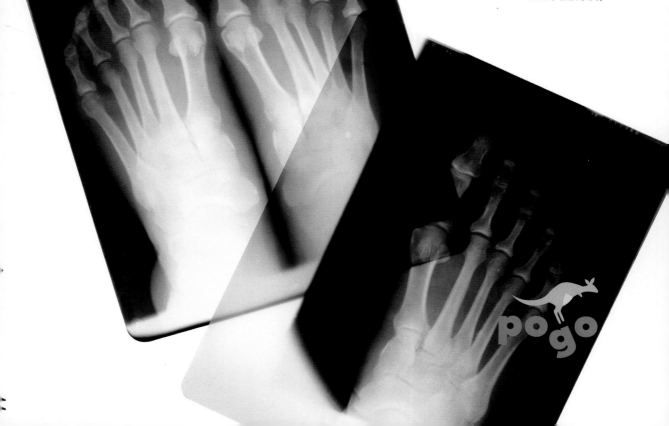

pogo

Ideas for Parents and Teachers

Pogo Books let children practice reading informational text while introducing them to nonfiction features such as headings, labels, sidebars, maps, and diagrams, as well as a table of contents, glossary, and index.

Carefully leveled text with a strong photo match offers early fluent readers the support they need to succeed.

Before Reading

- "Walk" through the book and point out the various nonfiction features. Ask the student what purpose each feature serves.
- Look at the glossary together. Read and discuss the words.

Read the Book

- Have the child read the book independently.
- Invite him or her to list questions that arise from reading.

After Reading

- Discuss the child's questions. Talk about how he or she might find answers to those questions.
- Prompt the child to think more. Ask: What other body systems do you know about? What do they do? How might they interact with the skeletal system?

Pogo Books are published by Jump!
5357 Penn Avenue South
Minneapolis, MN 55419
www.jumplibrary.com

Library of Congress Cataloging-in-Publication Data

Names: Kenney, Karen Latchana, author.
Title: Skeletal system / by Karen Latchana Kenney.
Description: Minneapolis, MN: Jump!, Inc. [2017]
Series: Amazing body systems
Audience: Ages 7-10.
Includes bibliographical references and index.
Identifiers: LCCN 2016035850 (print)
LCCN 2016036329 (ebook)
ISBN 9781620315620 (hardcover: alk. paper)
ISBN 9781620316023 (pbk.)
ISBN 9781624965104 (ebook)
Subjects: LCSH: Musculoskeletal system—Juvenile literature. | Human skeleton—Juvenile literature.
Classification: LCC QP301 .K46 2017 (print)
LCC QP301 (ebook) | DDC 612.7—dc23
LC record available at https://lccn.loc.gov/2016035850

Series Editor: Jenny Fretland VanVoorst
Series Designer: Anna Peterson
Photo Researcher: Anna Peterson

Photo Credits: All photos by Shutterstock except: Alamy, 10, 19; Dreamstime, 11; iStock, 3, 5, 6-7, 14-15, 16-17, 20-21.

Printed in the United States of America at Corporate Graphics in North Mankato, Minnesota.

TABLE OF CONTENTS

CHAPTER 1

INSIDE BONES

Can you jump high?
Can you ride a bike?
Can you stand straight
and tall?

Whatever you do with
your body, bones make
it possible.

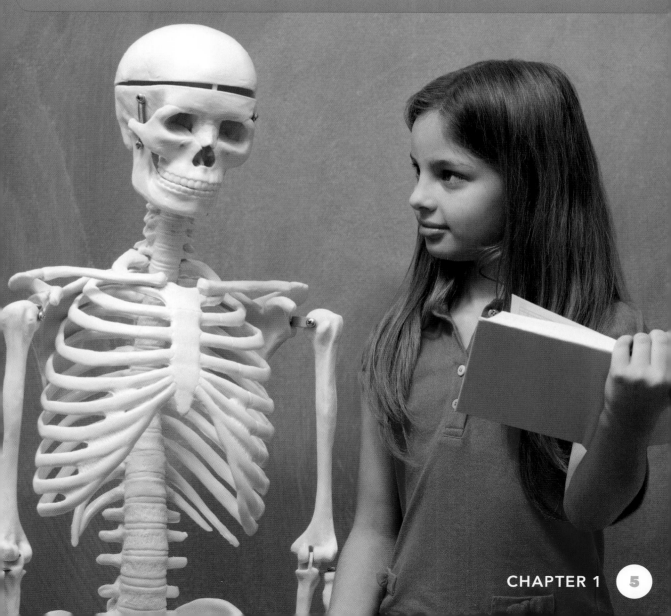

Bones make up your body's **skeletal system**. This system gives your body structure and support. It holds you up and helps you move. It also protects other **organs** of the body.

collagen

blood vessels

Bones are living tissue. They are made mostly of a material called **collagen**. They get blood from **blood vessels**. Blood gives energy to the **cells** inside.

The skeletal system is made of bones and **joints**.

skull

ribs

elbow

elbow

knee

knee

Bones have three layers. The hard outer layer is compact bone. Inside is spongy bone. It has many open spaces. Then comes the **marrow**, which is a bit like jelly. Some bones have red marrow. It's where blood cells are made. Other bones have yellow marrow. It stores fat.

DID YOU KNOW?

Bones store **minerals** the body needs, such as calcium.

spongy bone

marrow

compact bone

CHAPTER 2

YOUR SKELETON

Your skeleton is made up of 206 separate bones. Stretchy bands called **ligaments** hold them together.

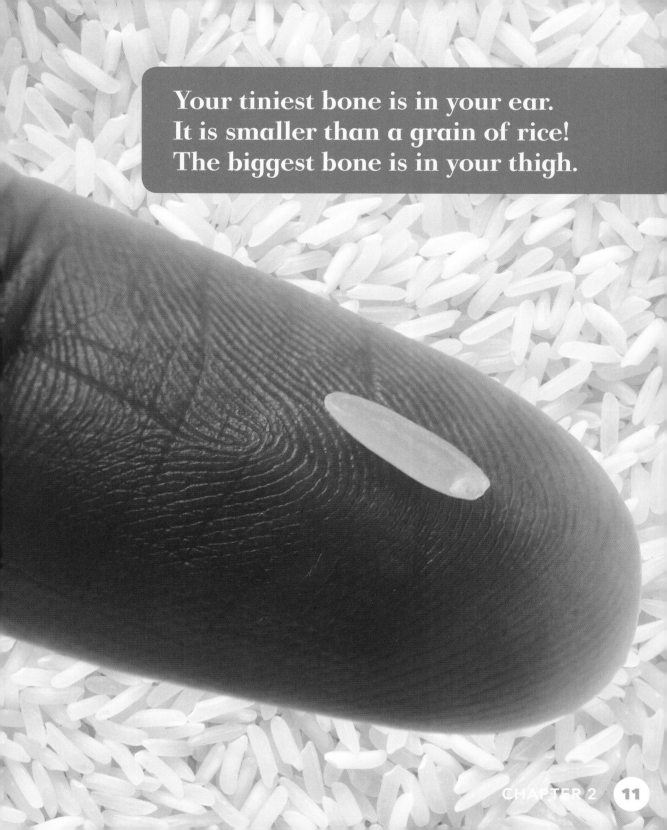

Your tiniest bone is in your ear.
It is smaller than a grain of rice!
The biggest bone is in your thigh.

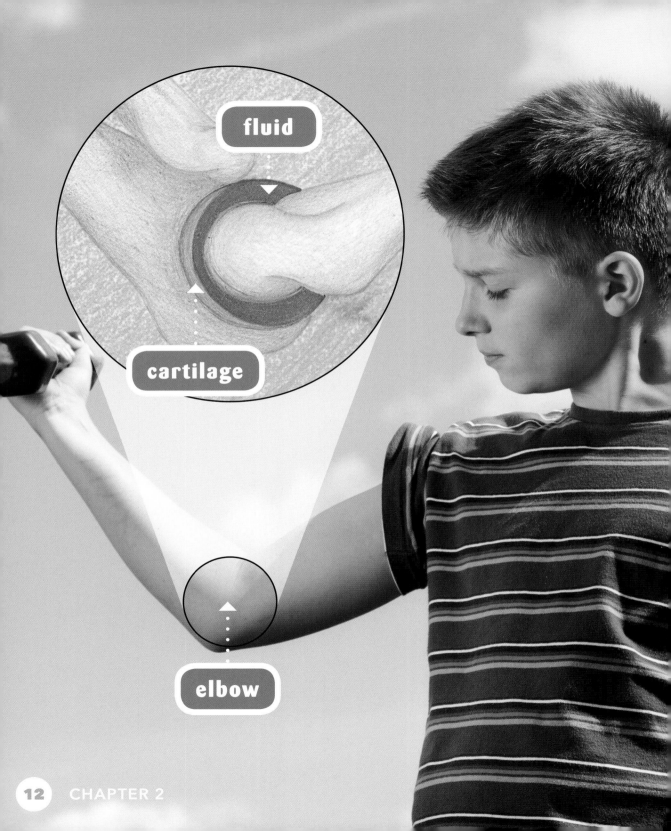

fluid

cartilage

elbow

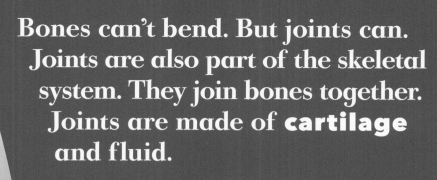

Bones can't bend. But joints can. Joints are also part of the skeletal system. They join bones together. Joints are made of **cartilage** and fluid.

Different joints move in different ways. Your elbow moves like a door hinge. It lets you bend and straighten your arm. Your wrist slides. It lets you move your hand up, down, and in a circle.

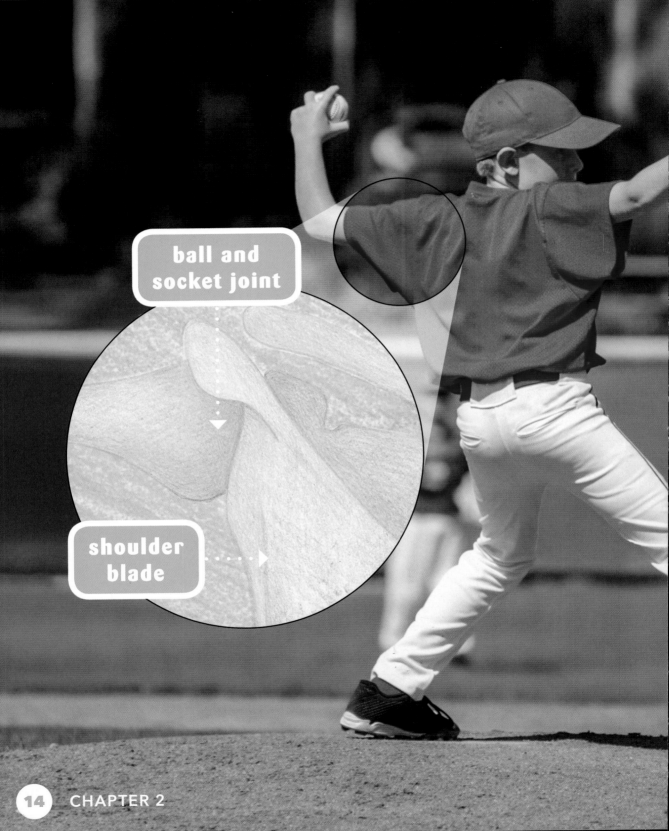

ball and
socket joint

shoulder
blade

Your upper arm connects with your shoulder blade. Between them is a ball and socket joint. It lets your arm move in all directions.

DID YOU KNOW?

A hand has 27 bones. A foot has 26. Together your hands and feet make up more than half the bones in your body!

Your bones wouldn't move without **muscles**. Stretchy **tendons** connect muscles with bones. When you want to move, your brain sends a message. It travels along **nerves** to a muscle. Then the muscle tightens to move your body.

Skeletal & Muscul

brain

CHAPTER 3

BODY ARMOR

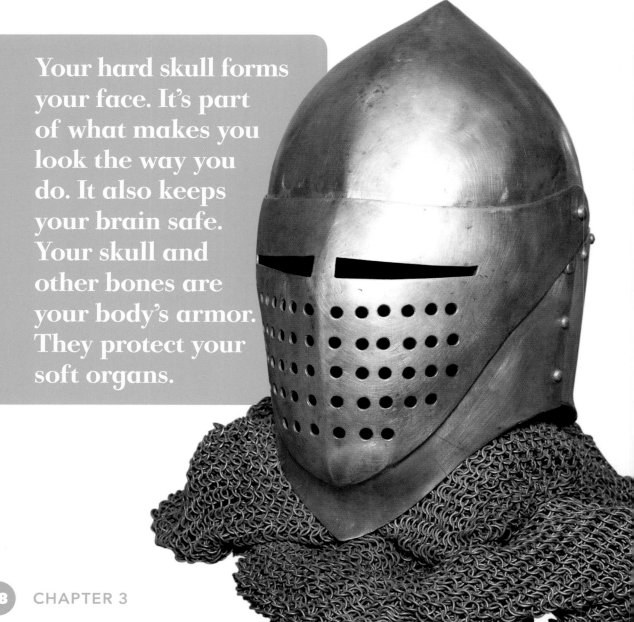

Your hard skull forms your face. It's part of what makes you look the way you do. It also keeps your brain safe. Your skull and other bones are your body's armor. They protect your soft organs.

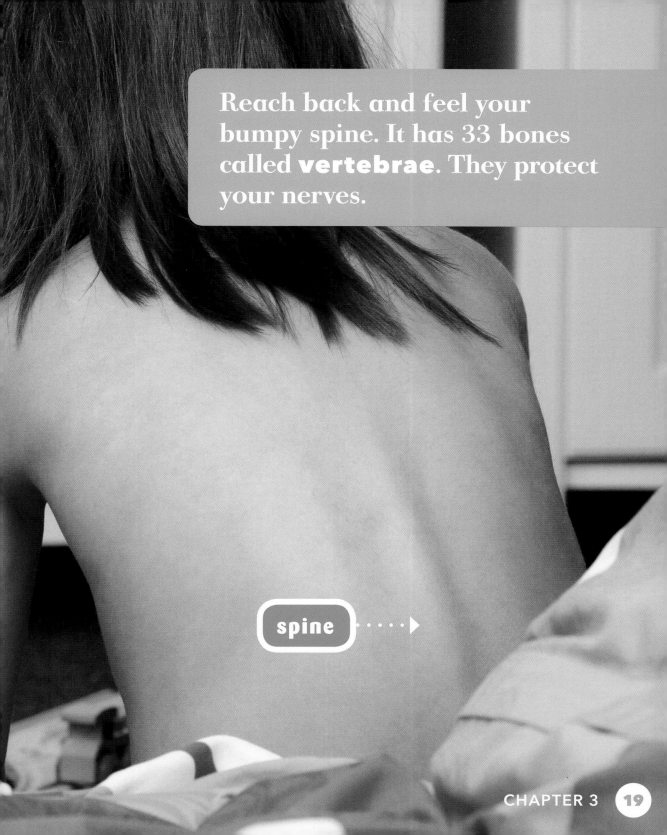

Reach back and feel your bumpy spine. It has 33 bones called **vertebrae**. They protect your nerves.

spine ·····▶

Inside your chest are your heart, lungs, and other organs. Your ribs surround them. Ribs connect with vertebrae. Joints along the spine let them move as you breathe.

Your skeletal system keeps your organs safe. It lets you stand straight and grow strong. It lets you run, jump, and climb. And it helps make you look like you!

DID YOU KNOW?

Your skeleton is always growing. Adults grow a mostly new set of bones every 10 years!

ACTIVITIES & TOOLS

TRY THIS!

BALL AND SOCKET JOINT

See how a ball and socket joint works in this activity.

What You Need:
- small paper cup
- modeling clay
- wooden craft stick

1. Roll a ball of modeling clay. Make sure it is a little smaller than the paper cup.

2. Place the ball in the cup. Stick the craft stick halfway into the ball.

3. Try moving the stick so that the ball moves. See which directions it can move.

GLOSSARY

blood vessels: Tubes that carry blood around the body.

cartilage: Strong tissue that connects bones.

cells: The basic building blocks of living things.

collagen: The primary structural material of the human body.

joints: Places where two or more bones meet.

ligaments: Tough bands of tissue that connect bones.

marrow: A soft substance inside bones where blood cells are made or fat is stored.

minerals: Naturally occurring substances that the body needs.

muscles: Tissue that connects to bones to make you move.

nerves: Threads of nerve cells that carry messages between the brain and the body.

organs: Parts of the body that do certain jobs.

skeletal system: The bones and joints that make up the frame of the body.

tendons: Stretchy, strong tissue that connects bones to muscles.

vertebrae: The small bones that make up the spine.

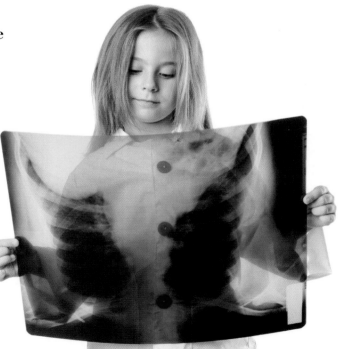

INDEX

TO LEARN MORE

Learning more is as easy as 1, 2, 3.

1) **Go to www.factsurfer.com**

2) **Enter "skeletalsystem" into the search box.**

3) **Click the "Surf" button to see a list of websites.**

With factsurfer, finding more information is just a click away.